Published by Creative Education
P.O. Box 227, Mankato, Minnesota 56002
Creative Education is an imprint of
The Creative Company
www.thecreativecompany.us

Design by The Design Lab
Production by Chelsey Luther
Art direction by Rita Marshall
Printed in the United States of America

Photographs by Corbis (Tim Davis), Dreamstime
(Steve Byland, Gregg Williams), Getty Images
(Susan Gary, Visuals Unlimited Inc./Adam Jones),
Shutterstock (Pedro Bernardo, Charles Brutlag, Dec
Hogan, KellyNelson), SuperStock (Exactostock,
Minden Pictures, Tier und Naturfotografie, Radius,
Universal Images Group)

Library of Congress Cataloging-in-Publication Data
Riggs, Kate.
Hummingbirds / Kate Riggs.
p. cm. — (Amazing animals)
Summary: A basic exploration of the appearance,
behavior, and habitat of hummingbirds, Earth's small-
est birds. Also included is a story from folklore ex-
plaining why hummingbirds have beautiful feathers.
Includes bibliographical references and index.
ISBN 978-1-60818-348-7
1. Hummingbirds—Juvenile literature. I. Title. II.
Series: Amazing animals.

QL696.A558R54 2014
598.7'64—dc23   2013002865

9 8 7 6 5 4 3 2

AMAZING ANIMALS

HUMMINGBIRDS

BY KATE RIGGS

CREATIVE EDUCATION

Hummingbirds

are the smallest birds in the world. There are more than 300 kinds of hummingbirds! Many hummingbirds live in South America. But some live in North and Central America, too.

Female ruby-throated hummingbirds do not have a red throat

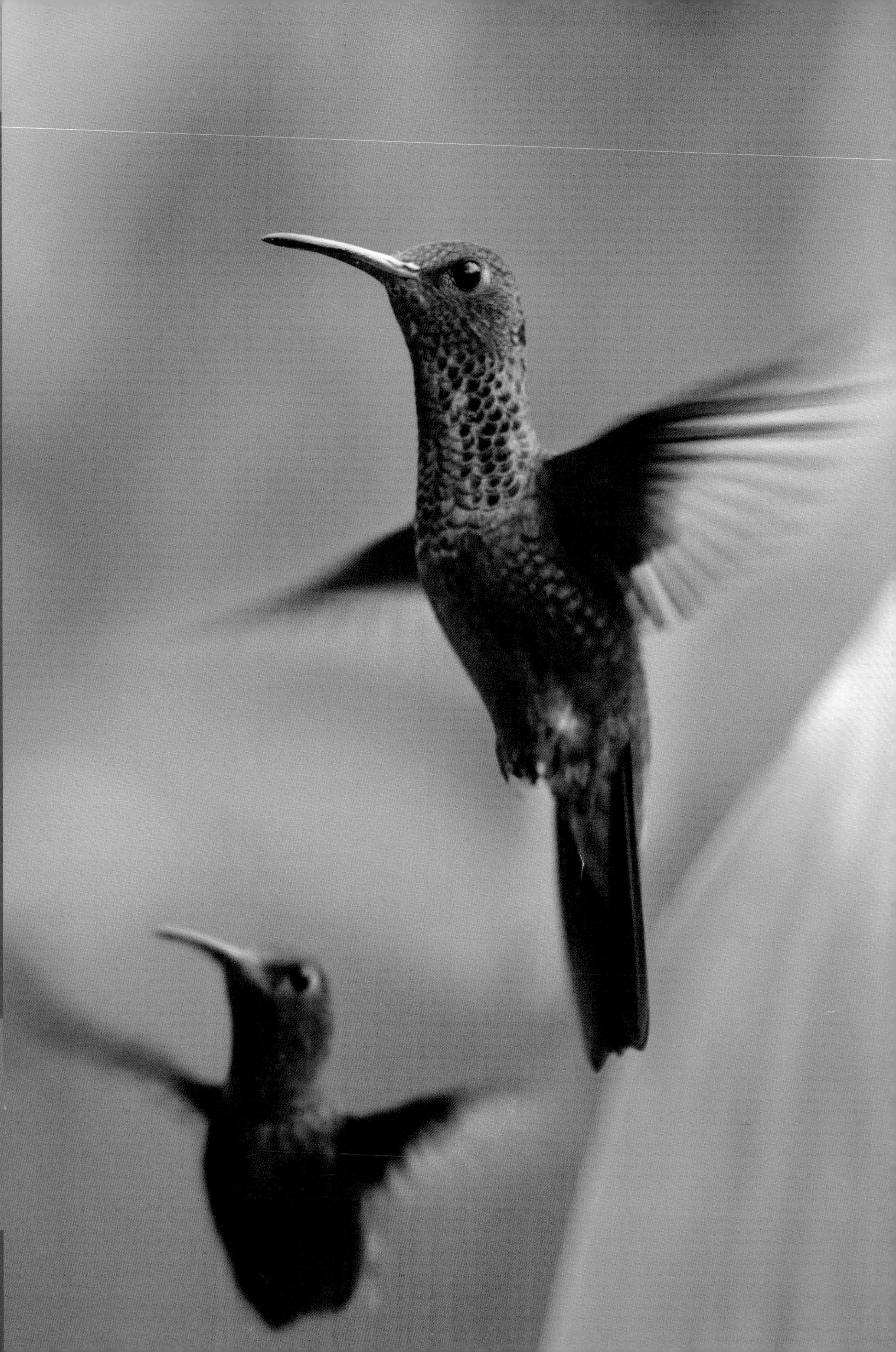

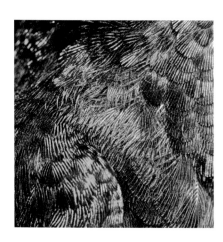

Hummingbirds have about 1,000 feathers on their body

Hummingbirds

have colorful feathers. They have a long, pointy **beak**. Hummingbirds fly so fast that their wings make a humming sound. That is how they got their name.

beak the part of a bird's mouth that sticks out from its face

The smallest hummingbirds weigh less than a penny! Their bodies are only one inch (2.5 cm) long. The largest hummingbirds weigh about as much as six sheets of paper. These hummingbirds are more than eight inches (20.3 cm) long.

Rufous hummingbirds (opposite) are 4 inches (10.2 cm) long

Most hummingbirds live in the warmest parts of the Americas. Many hummingbirds in North America **migrate** south in the winter. They go where they can find the most food.

migrate   move from place to place to find food and warmth

*A hummingbird eats five
to eight times per hour*

Hummingbirds

eat insects and food from flowers.
The **nectar** made by flowers is sweet.
Hummingbirds need to eat a lot of sugary
nectar. A hummingbird uses its curved
beak and long tongue to reach the nectar
inside a flower.

nectar a sweet, sugary liquid that flowers make

A hummingbird egg is less than 0.5 inch (1.3 cm) long

A female hummingbird builds a nest before laying two eggs. She keeps the eggs warm until they **hatch**. Baby hummingbirds eat food their mother brings to them. Hummingbirds leave the nest when they are about one month old.

hatch break open

Many hummingbirds live about four to six years. Snakes and big birds called kestrels try to catch and eat hummingbirds. Hummingbirds live close to other hummingbirds. But they do not live together in families.

Hummingbirds scoot sideways but do not hop or walk

A hummingbird flaps its wings 50 to 200 times per second

Hummingbirds

feed and fly all day. They are the only birds that can fly in any direction. They fly up, down, forwards, and backwards. They can even **hover**! Hummingbirds eat a lot of food so that they can fly.

hover stay in one place in the air

Sometimes you can see hummingbirds at special bird feeders. People can make a sugary water that hummingbirds like. It is fun to watch these colorful birds dart through the air!

Some feeders have spots where birds can perch

Why are hummingbirds' feathers so beautiful? People in Mexico told a story about this. The hummingbird used to be plain and gray. But she was cheerful and helpful. She had many bird friends. Her friends gave her some of their colorful feathers to make a wedding dress. The hummingbird loved the dress so much that she wore it forever. Hummingbirds are still some of the prettiest birds.

Read More

Kalz, Jill. *Hummingbirds*. North Mankato, Minn.: Smart Apple Media, 2002.

Sill, Cathryn. *About Hummingbirds*. Atlanta: Peachtree, 2011.

Websites

Activity TV: Hummingbird Feeder
http://www.activitytv.com/306-hummingbird-feeder
Watch this video and have an adult help you make a hummingbird feeder!

Hummingbird Puzzles, Quizzes, & Coloring Pages
http://www.rubythroat.org/ActivitiesPuzzlesMain.html
Do a fun activity and learn more about ruby-throated hummingbirds.

Index

Americas 4, 11
beaks 7, 12
eggs 15
feathers 7, 22
feeders 20
flying 7, 19

food 11, 12, 15, 19
migration 11
nests 15
predators 16
sizes 8
tongues 12